Random Experiments in Bioluminescence is a remarkable collection of luminous poems for cherishing cultures, languages, and the Earth — From poet and urbanist Dr. Amy Shimshon-Santo.

"Listen with your natural body," writes Shimshon-Santo. "In the beginning, there was song." This collection tracks a woman's search for language and belonging. Choral, cryptographic, and exhilarating, Shimshon-Santo provides glimpses into a poetics of planetary livability.

The collection opens with a "genealogy of the moment" in "x or x prime clock time." Trees and vines "tangle their hair together" to escape over brick walls. A piano decomposes into forest mulch. Seaweed fronds curl around pilings. Gravity "plants humans in the ground like oaks" while black birds murmurate skyward. Echolocate in the galaxy through poems, and become a "rapture gawker of infinity consciousness."

Mother tongues join a line dance of translations with family and friends. A trilingual villanelle for òrìṣà cohabitates with talmudic inspired piyyut. Poems morph into flow charts, pictograms, haikus, and chants — scattered between photographs of habitats.

Her verse has kinesthetic momentum on the page—flowing from right to left or left to right, ascending or descending, to weave conversations between languages. The outcome of *Random Experiments in Bioluminescence* is a homecoming to the body and the planet; respect for multiple languages and awe for life in our pluriverse.

Praise for
Random Experiments in Bioluminescence

"Shimshon-Santo's humor bubbles through this collection, along with her wisdom—"Eekspay Achurnay?" she asks us in Pig Latin, bringing playfulness to the table, and indeed, she plays with form throughout, bringing in mathematical equations and cryptography and photography, leaving out vowels, sharing a dream in an exhilarating rush of ellipses. Words dance across the page. These pages bring us back to our most embodied, enmeshed selves, bring us back to the Earth and its abundant wonders."

—Gayle Brandeis (*Drawing Breath*)

"Amy Shimshon-Santo is the most organic poet I have ever read. Her polylingualism extends beyond our species, feeding us meaning from panoramic angles. Language is simply the stuff she inhales and exhales. Like a spell in the stern, nurturing lap of Mother Earth."

—Mamle Wolo (*Flying Through Water*)

"Amy Shimshon-Santo's poetry is an exploration of the deeper connections between the selves and identities molded by languages, cultures, and the land(s) we inhabit. The poems weave the tragedies we experience daily with the beauty and wonderment of being alive. Among separation and closeness, desperation and hope, Shimshon-Santo offers us the gift of inhabiting these spaces in the present moment. She invites us to listen to and to thrive in the abundance that is all around us."

— Leonora Simonovis (*Study of the Raft*)

"Amy Shimshon-Santo's poems are the words of a survivor, a warrior, and a creator. Time and time again, across borders and languages, her writing takes us into sensuous and deeply emotional places, finding beauty and rootedness and meaning in everyday moments and extraordinary landscapes.

—Héctor Tobar (*Our Immigrant Souls*)

RANDOM EXPERIMENTS IN BIOLUMINESCENCE

Amy Shimshon-Santo

Flowersong Press Aztlan

FLOWERSONG
PRESS

Published by Flowersong Press
www.flowersong press.com

Library of Congress Cataloguing-in-Publication Data

Name: Amy Shimshon-Santo
Title: Random Experiments in Bioluminescence
Description: Poetry
Identifiers: LCCN 2024944171
ISBN: 978-1-963245-35-6
Subjects: Poetry, Languages, Habitat, Ecology, Pluriverse

Cover Art by Pao Chutijirawong
Book Design by Amy Shimshon-Santo
Author Photograph by Bobby Gordon
Set in Garamond Premier Pro and Helvetica

Printed in the Unites States of America

Other Titles by Amy Shimshon-Santo

POETRY

Catastrophic Molting

Even the Milky Way is Undocumented

Endless Bowls of Sky

ANTHOLOGIES

Corpos, gêneros e literatura de autoria feminina
with Ana Rita Santiago & Tatiana Pequeno

Et Al.: New Voices in Arts Management
with Genevieve Kaplan

Arts = Education

Get your bearings. Hear the trees.

—C.D. Wright

Everything, everyone, is empty of a separate existence.
Therefore to take care of the other is to take care of oneself.
To take care of the trees is to take care of oneself.
To take care of the river is to take care of oneself.
Because a self is made of non-self atoms.

—Thich Nhat Hanh

CONTENTS

POLLINATION

PROXIMITY

¾ OF OUR SURFACE

UNDERGROWTH

GRAVITATIONAL FIELDS

Árvore Geneológica do Momento
Árbol Geneológico del Momento
Geneological Tree of the Moment

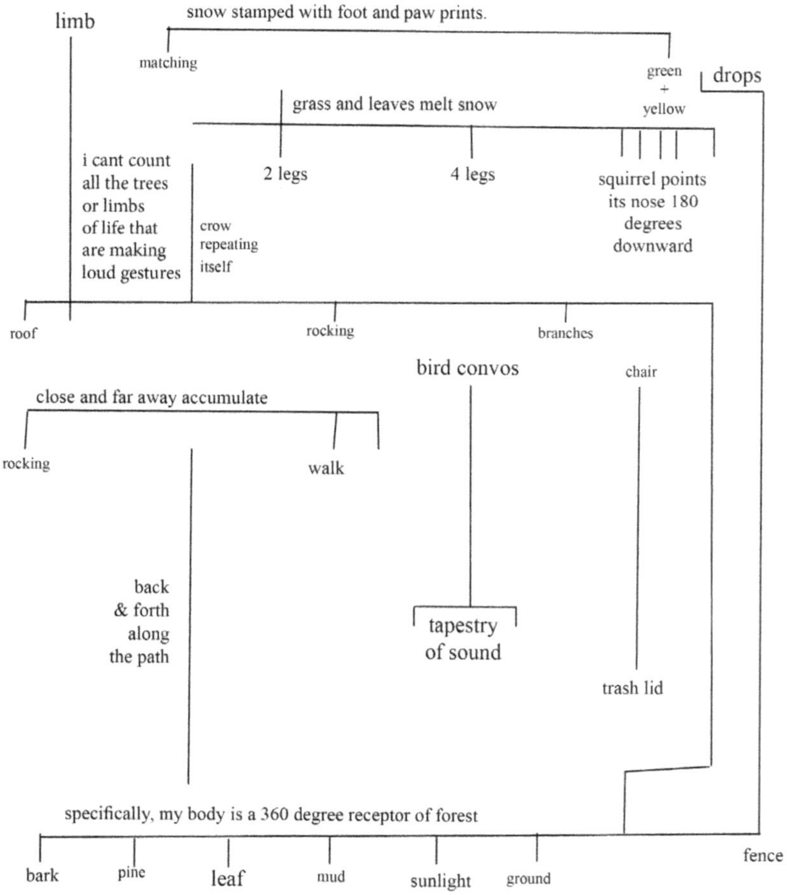

limb
snow stamped with foot and paw prints.
matching
green + yellow
drops
grass and leaves melt snow
2 legs
4 legs
squirrel points its nose 180 degrees downward
i cant count all the trees or limbs of life that are making loud gestures
crow repeating itself
roof
rocking
branches
bird convos
chair
close and far away accumulate
rocking
walk
back & forth along the path
tapestry of sound
trash lid
specifically, my body is a 360 degree receptor of forest
bark
pine
leaf
mud
sunlight
ground
fence

INTRODUCTION

By Gayle Brandeis

"(L)isten with your natural body," Amy Shimshon-Santo instructs at the start of Random Experiments in Bioluminescence, and this deep, expansive book indeed requires—and deserves—whole body listening. These pages brim with chirr and hum and burble, teem with the vitality and play and beauty (and, sometimes, brutality) of the more-than-human-world we all belong to. These pages bring us back to our most embodied, enmeshed selves, bring us back to the Earth and its abundant wonders.

Shimshon-Santo's breathtaking previous collection, *Catastrophic Molting*, was born of grief—a full-throated, love-anchored cry against racialized violence, against human atrocity. *Random Experiments in Bioluminescence* chronicles the healing that deep, intentional grounding in nature can bring, even in the midst of despair. As she writes in her Acknowledgements, "Writing with nature is not an escape. It is a return." These poems invite us to return with her, to join her in becoming "rapture-gawker of fresh infinity consciousness."

A polylingual poet, Shimshon-Santo celebrates the multiplicity of tongues—human and beyond, on our planet—translating her own work into Spanish, Portuguese, Enna/Mazateco, Hebrew, Arabic, Twi, Hñähñu, Tagalog, Japanese, and Ancient Chinese with the help of friends and family, turning her own voice communal, choral, while also translating millipede and ocean and black bird into English, distilling the symphony of the natural world into her singular voice. "Loan me language so I can return it to you," she asks Edge of the Lake, Freshwater Marsh, Bulrush, Alkaline Flat. "Praise the endless landed languages of here!"

Her humor bubbles through this collection, along with her wisdom—"Eekspay Achurnay?" she asks us in Pig Latin, bringing playfulness to the table, and indeed, she plays with form throughout, bringing in mathematical equations and cryptography and photography, leaving out vowels, sharing a dream in an exhilarating rush of ellipses. Words dance across the page in this collection in a dynamic variety of shapes, echoing Shimshon-Santo's background as a professional dancer. "I am letting light, sound & words swarm the page," she writes, and this swarm is palpable—the light and sound and words fly right off the page, and lift us with them, so we, as readers, become part of their murmuration.

1.

Pollination

i stolisten to the teninsects
and shedbirds their rrrrrr-rr
chep, brrrrwirl

INCUNABULA SONOGRAFICA

tree trunks grow in clusters
circling parking lots & dumpsters

I leave the container to take in all the action
listen with my natural body

to the chi, chi, chi, caw, brrrrriiiiiit
ta ti-ta-ti-ta-ti-ta-ti-symphony of wind & feathers

in the beginning,
there was song

EARTHLING ADDRESS

> I prefer, to their dogma, my excursions
> into the natural gardens where the voice
> of the Great Spirit is heard in the twitter of birds,
> the rippling of mighty waters, and the sweet
> breathing of flowers ... If this is Paganism,
> then, at present at least, I am a Pagan.
> —Zitkala Sa (1876 - 1938)

Dear Butterflies,
Buzzy Pollen Flowers,
Hummingbirds,
Hybrid Swarms,
Pollen,
Sphinx Moths,
Nectar Tubes,
Pygmy Nuthatch,

Hello.

Beloved Magma deep in the earth's core,
Honorable Granite, Quartz & Dilate,
Esteemed Silica and Volcanic Rock,

Thank you for the ground we stand on.
I will become more deep mixing pollinator,
more lodgepole, more conifer forest
than superstitious cataract of capitalism.

Wonderful Wasps,
Aphids,
and Weird Shaped Flowers,

Hear me.
This geographical snapshot is a legacy
of fire and culture suppression.

Help me inhabit longer time frames,
honor centuries of weather-wise societies,
molding life and style with the seasons
in multidimensional microclimates.

Esteemed Storm Water and Winter,

Help me phenologically
so dawn can be a chorus of birds in June
before the leaf-out spring, people-less Octobers,
and stark Februaries buried in snow motion;
so aviary passage migrants can stay safe in numbers
singing community protection songs.

Dear Edge of the Lake,
Freshwater Marsh,
Bulrush,
Alkaline Flat,

Loan me language so I can return it to you.
Let me learn the words for non-destroy ability.
Incubate them on my tongue.
Praise the endless landed languages of here.

PROFANITY

—after Gerald Stern

I like the way light and shadow mosaic the ground
I like hearing birds cussing even if I can't see who said what
I like the scraggly tangerine blossoms
I watch the electric pole pierce the sky
I listen to the morning through my eyes
I sit between dream life and Thursday
I walk my pencil through notebook leaves
I let light, sound, and words swarm the page

SELF PORTRAIT AS TWO HUMMINGBIRDS

self portrait as time inside a body
self portrait as a fire pit
self portrait as tomato plant
self portrait as wood chips
self portrait as pencil
self portrait as a ravaged red prickly pear discarded in the dirt
self portrait as wilting rose bushes
self portrait as digestion
self portrait as deep breathing
self portrait as an orchestra of crows

ART + LABOR

artists always have work
    but don't always have a job,
food, or a place to stay,
    don't always have supplies
but always have material,
    don't always have money
but labor incessantly

we always have something to do,
    investigate, learn, know
say, always translating life
    into new forms, awakening
and dreaming, alone
    and in communion

artists seize opportunities
    for living, leave "positions"
to do the real work
    of making culture,
histories, futures, a present
    worth participating in

we labor in the days
    and in the nights,
in a job you don't apply for
    that never leaves you,
work that changes
    and connects lifetimes

creation is a necessary endeavor
— sit on the land at the feet of humanity
saying speak to me   speak to me
I am listening

ARTE + LABOR [es]

artistas siempre tienen trabajo
    pero no siempre tienen empleo,
comida, o un lugar para quedarse,
    no siempre tienen recursos
pero siempre tienen material,
    no siempre tienen dinero
pero trabajan incesantemente

siempre tenemos algo que hacer,
    investigar, aprender, saber,
decir, traduciendo la vida
    en nuevas formas, despertando
y soñando, solos
    y en comunión

artistas agarran oportunidades
    para vivir, dejan "posiciones"
para realizar el trabajo real
    de hacer cultura,
historias, futuros, un presente
    que valga la pena participar

trabajamos en los días
    y en las noches
en mano de obra que no se candidata
    y que nunca te deja,
trabajo que transforma
    y conecta vidas

creación es un esfuerzo necesario
— sentarse en la tierra, al pie de la humanidad
diciendo, cuéntame   cuéntame
            estoy escuchando

ARTE + LABOR [po]

artistas sempre têm trabalho
    mas nem sempre têm emprego,
comida, ou lugar para ficar
    nem sempre têm recursos
mas sempre têm material
    nem sempre têm dinheiro
mas trabalham incessantemente

sempre temos algo para fazer,
    investigar, aprender, saber
dizer, sempre traduzindo vidas
em novas formas
acordando e sonhando, sozinhos
e em comunhão

artistas agarram oportunidades
    para viver, deixam "posições"
para realizar o trabalho real
    de fazer cultura,
histórias, futuros, e um presente
    que vale a pena participar

trabalhamos dias e noites
    em mão de obra para o qual
não se candidata
    e que nunca te deixa,
trabalho que transforma
    e conecta vidas

criação ê um esforço necessário
— sente-se na terra, ao pé da humanidade
dizendo, conte-me   conte-me
    eu estou ouvindo

2.

Proximity

0.

day after day
after lockdown day
germinating silence.
beyond a dirty window,
the rotund full moon
is luminous, round
as an aspirin pill

POTENTIAL LIVABILITY

even when the psalm
reads “there is a net and pestilent hole
dug for our capture by flaming lions”

we shelter beneath the open wings of our neshuma
crochet patience from recycled thread
stretch elbows in 33 directions
step into the night
recognize each day
plunge thumb after thumb, into the dark earth
illuminated by the moon’s silver

breath inflates and exhalates the lungs
while birds sleep in floating branches

MAKE THE BODY STAY

her hand zip-zaps eyes transmitting data in a dot-dash-dot kind of way the hair along her arm, erect from the chill of unconfined air filtering through the window screen. ambidextrous, she guides a pencil with her right, and slugs a glass of warmth with her left she would be categorized a righty, leaning on her left side hip bone against the woven rug, bones balancing her three dimensionality on the floor, bipedal, two gangly legs a set of knees and ankles bouquets of bones called feet or pes, like the plastic dispenser candy, it was time again for paper dolls and toys small things she could manipulate unlike the big things that were stuck, destroyed, off center or phenomenally unwell, she rests her left cheek on her left hand of her left knee left pondering what to write, her eyes land on a pile of blue masks stationed on a wooden table one bent like a tiny tent the other stretched out like a sleeping bag for mice

away, away, away is what she wished. stay, stay, stay is what she did.

TOPOGRAPHICAL YES MAP

.

meditative set up

four blank stanzas

composition of place

inward journey

un-conclusion

.

THE SAVIORS OF A SOLITARY CYCLE

are bees

pollinating fluorescent

flowers, communing

with birds & red

orb weavers

are bees

pollinating fluorescent

flowers, communing

with birds & red

orb weavers

WEATHER

a sparrow careens through an opening in the orange tree branches
yellow-white citrus blossoms fandango

I witness the extravagant saga of the life cycle
from a frame being devoured by termites

put on a fluorescent yellow shirt
pitch a rickety chair by the lemon tree

the solution to a cage is outside
better than a window is a door

weeds comfort the soil
everything knows it's about to rain

the clouds are summoning a downpour
while I am conjuring spring

HERE

→

shift focus from catastrophes
to crickets and crows
find out how to live
inside the smallest moment of your history,
your task is to breathe

→

enter the garden barefoot
make yourself useful
find the tangled coil of a green hose
babble with the birds perched on electric wires
click your tongue w/ gray sparrows
& blur-winged hummingbirds

imagine your body a small sanctuary
away from the everyday banality
& outright degradation
of profound change

→

the crown of my head
is sister to the carrot stub
growing upside down
in the dirt

←

a line is one long breath
the spider's black eyelash legs
climb liquid air
dangling from invisible thread

←

keep still,

a yellow jacket hovers
by my left pinky finger
it does not attack

MULTIPLE SPECIES

I find a single prayer and it is not for men. —W.S. Merwin

apple, blood orange, fig, lemon, apricot, palm
persimmon, peach, avocado

we're in a pod with rosemary, agave, purple sage

one wild iris & two fast ants searching stucco

airplane exhaust lines the actually blue sky

blow on a spider & it curls into a ball

beneath electric wires thorny antlers cover the rose bush

I peel off all my clothes to gobble up the light

100s of days pass

all of us circling the fireball planet

GARDEN OF LETTERS

A

powerless to the socio-gigantor
ecology commands my attention
earth is a laboratory

B

it doesn't matter what i think
life will grow where it wants

C

bees and bugs approve
birds believe this garden is the place to be

D

i dig a hole in the ground for the jerusalem sage
it withers in the shade, thin roots need more space
so i replant its existence in full light
inside a generous split barrel
life can survive multiple migrations

E

a woman of the city, i've no green thumb
but as i fill containers with soil & plants
they tell me how they are and what they want

F

not here. yes there.
be patient. pay attention.

G

fingernails mooned with dirt
skin of the hands speckled
with wounds that are healing

H

mint and oregano quiver in the wind
when the wooden chair comes apart
I pound it's slats back together

I

surrounded by piles of dried plant detritus
wilted tubes of blossom-less calla lilies
tangled fireworks of purple sage

J

a fallen orange rots on the ground
mauled by a squirrel
split open
alone by the rain gutter

K

oregano sees what happened to the mint
they're in the same family
one has a ceramic pot and the other does not
there are not enough pots or planters for all the ideas

L

bees and bugs hover around me
and the rosy red valerian
they wonder if I am pollinateable

M

if bugs have plants and plants have hummingbirds,
what do I have?

N

if I sit still enough beside the lemon tree
4 feet from the fig
90 degrees from the lavender
what will I grow into?

O

i've become attached to chrysanthemums
wed to an avocado tree
kissing coral roses to begin each day anew

P

the rake, hoe, and shovel
lined up along the brick wall
are the guardians of this small verdant space

Q

plants keep reaching out to each other
spinning tendrils weave a tangled coexistence
they wrap their hair together

R

the tree & the vine make a perfect team
accomplices in the act
green crawlers scale the apricot tree
the vine crochets its branches
they escape over the wall

curling around the light post
ignoring the city's parking placard

S

a beanstalk will finally
reach the clouds
to extinguish the giant

T

the city sends me a memo
demanding I cut down the overgrowth
I'm required to obey the jurisdictions of my species
so I hack, cut, gather, and compost

U

i climb the wall with gloved hands and a saw
limbs, branches, and leaves
collapse onto the sidewalk
filling the gutter

V

i drill silver wire into the wall for the vine to cling to
please leave the tree alone

W

now, they are with each other
but are not each other

X

i've been writing plants
insects, birds, and dried amber leaves

while the sweet h sapiens are sounds
emitted from a screen
and the broken ones are warring

Y

with any luck
the people will enjoy an explosion of tenderness
when the harmfulness is contained in a dumpster

Z

meanwhile, i am here
watching the vine dance in the breeze
and the avocado leaves rumble

1000 BIRD TREE

Let me stop singing and tell you about this brown twig. We are migrants from the 1000 bird tree that was massacred last year when the humans cut down our world. They've killed most of the trees around here. Our singing trees are gone, and singing is what we like to do. What you call singing we call living. Human homes aren't even alive, and they cannibalize space. Now, there aren't enough homes for all the humans, and the rest of us are squatters. When they massacred the 1000 bird tree we migrated south in search of good branches, limbs, and leaves; good bushes and flowers. We are many. We hop and scrape our feet in the dirt. I'm lucky to be able to rest in the peach tree. There are seeds and dried leaves and grass for making nests. There are more sparrows than people. A woman lives here too. She has no wings; not one single feather. When the sun returns she comes outside to be with us, and sits in a chair. I watch her from a branch and click. She doesn't shoo us away, or cut down the vines and trees. People make such strange sounds. Who knows what they're trying to sing? We, on the other wing, make music: rhythmic clicking tapestries, feathers fluttering open and shut like fans. Humans might call it morse code, but we're not warring birds. This is how we make the world beautiful. If I sang to you, you wouldn't know how to read it.

Everyday, we sing our culture, jokes, and games.
Everyday, you think: chirping.

1000 BIRD TREE

Mek me stop to dey sing for now tell you one or two about dis tree. We be dem 1000 bird tree wey dem massacre last year wey man dem pursue us for awa home. Dem almost done kill all dem tree for here. Dem trees wey dey sing done go, & you sef suppose sabe say singing na di ting wey we sabe do. Wetin you sef call music na how we dey take live. No be even say man dem home dey breathe, dem just sabe chop space. We dey drag space wit dem because dem no even get enof for dem sef. Wen dem been butcher di 1000 bird tree, we begin movement reach south make we for see beta place to hang do awa ting. We plenty. We dey jollificate for detty. Me sef get luck say I see one peach tree to rest. Dis place get plenty tings wey we go fit use make awa home. For here we get sparrows pass man. One woman live for here sef. She no even get wings, she no get feather. She dey come siddon wit us wen di sun komot. Me, wen I see am I go begin sing. She no dey bother us. She no dey reason cut dem trees. Di sound pipo mek funny me pass. Who sabe di kain ting wey dem dey sing? We wey get wings sabe dis music ting all through to di way awa wings dey beat for sky. Pipo dey call am morse code, but no be we dey go war kill person. Na like dis we dey carry paint dis world mek e fine. If I sing give you, you no go fit sabe am.

Everyday, we gather sing awa ting.
Everyday, you tink say na noise.

Translated into Nigerian Pidgin by Àkpà Árinzèchukwu

LEMON | LIMÓN

1. abundance is a lemon tree
laden with green, yellow
citrus evolutioning
reaching skyward
becoming branches beaded
by fruit, bending
toward its own earth

2. the tree I live with turns sunshine into citrus
co2 > oxygen
my address is árvore
kin to los colibrí
antidote & conqueror of colds
inspiration for myriad cups of tea
hot lemonade bavarka remedies
passed down generations
citron-aroma for your body
to cure almost anything

3. I reside inside a lemon tree
that's why my mother visits me
may I come get lemons?
mom stands beside the tree
it's so happy here, she chirps

once she arrived unannounced
pushed open the wooden gate
plucked as many fruit as she could carry
in the soft bowl of her t-shirt
then, departed cooing over her harvest
ogling the yellow-yellow-yellow
all the while, oblivious to me watching

4. I have witnessed the invention of a lemon
dreamt of watching the city from its branches
fruit fall, ferment, renew
pistils floral microexplosion
delicate citric-intentions
dark green grenades
clustered celebrations of color
not to be confused with grapefruit
when they over do it
aromatic heaven, ah
yum, mmm, ooooh
haha-amazing

5. before there was the fruit called lemon-limón
landing on your kitchen table
there was a limb, a trunk, a tree growing skyward
from underground splash of reaching roots,
the origin of a lemon is árbol-universo

FIG KNUCKLES

after 5 years of knee-high existence
the fig tree identified
a source of groundwater

count 1-2-3
4-5-6 7-8-9-10
11-12-13-14-15-16-17-18 leaves
the size of mouse fans
castanet fingers & hands

& one green stub
of its very-first-fruit!

Botanical Update: After this fig tree poem was written, the neighboring grape arbor expanded and cannibalized the sunshine. The fig tree lay down and crawled on the ground in search of its own light. When I realized what was going on, I clipped back the vine, supported the fig tree's limbs, and added new earth around its base. As of this writing, the fig is upright and there are enough sunbeams for all.

HOW TO EAT A TREE

spin the orange ball
hold it to your nose
breathe in the sharp scent

rip off the nib
tear back the rind
expose the soft inner pith

> > bite < <

wet color splatters
squint your eyes shut
take in the tang

kabang-baludang
on your tongue
taste the gallop of spring

MURMURATION

in the joy of a dream, I levitate in the tree canopy
but when I awake, gravity is my anchor

all the human dwellings are on the ground
sheltering land-bound bodies

black birds dance above the rooftops
crackling sounds in the fresh morning

I run to the window, so does the child across the street
exploding from his door onto the sidewalk

our arms open in chorus, wide as wings
while we witness the splendor of black birds flocking

shimshon, the birds want to be watched and heard
our bodies listen, planted in the ground like oaks

RESIDENCE

I reside   .   with the dried leaves

        .

        clustered on

                the earth   .

beneath   a grove of pines .

        our names   .

        known   .   only to loved ones

                        not   the forgetting machine

                that spins

        :   each soul   around

        pointing it

                                away from its roots

TERRESTRE

yo convivo . junto con las hojas secas verde oliva

.

unidas en

la tierra

debajo de una alameda de pinos .

nuestros nombres

son reconocidos . solamente por los seres queridos

no la máquina del olvido

que gira

: cada alma dando vueltas

apuntándola

lejos de sus raíces

GUAA' 'VÖ

kóó kánma sééa . kóó' ma' mo

röö' mo'

ni guaa' 'vö .

la' në' kóó mo' li sä 'ma kïï .

e sii jnää' . jíí' dzä í . í in jnääbaa'

likuii

jó fa ñi e ga, e jmi in dzi .

mï jíí

: jmï ngan dzi dzä

tiin

víí koti li sén dzä

Chinanteco translation by E. Xagaat García

SHABBAT CRYPTOGRAM

7565-487 47t7t1-6`-
a woman holds a scissors
a thimble and a measuring tape
9[2758? 24872303456 49081
487 4457887 678482> < 374@54577611384848
where are you headed? I ask
to measure the soul of the city she says
to know how tall and wide it will be
894 8) q648487 47t7t7t75489574 || 8585758
13577565-487 47t7t1-6`-5==`=6`5
the sun hides behind a white bolt of clouds
wind shakes the trees rippling our heavy skirts
8875&^% 459 87677694 30914716* (40914
487 901300092865 439303=- 7ru
the seamstress rushes past
silver needle glimmering in her hand
9378003 -7546784834487 64200 94651
38 .576793 9349 ---- #. ^ 597t49t 99030
run after her, says the wind
tell her the city shall have no walls
it will be home to all living things
678482> < 374@54577487 74 || 858575 01439

REMOTE / INCANDESCENT

it is father's day
but mine is now an ancestor
I mark time passing with time inside a tent
portable hotplate
collapsible pot for boiling water

but blingification notches this campsite
evidence of families means monster RVs
with 8-wheeled bike racks
see-through rip-stop temporal habitations

while the campground snores
my tortoise shell bones are awake
horizontal inside a sleeping sack
floating an inch above the earth
on an inflatable orange pad

my skin is protected
from 23 degree snow-melt air
but the body has to piss
I spend hours deciding how to approach this reality
coach myself to hold it in,
psych myself up to go outside
& wet a stone like any other mammal

I finally enter the night
& there it is
— our galaxy glaring down at me
beyond the ring of towering tree silhouettes
crisp-speckled light
sears through the sky's maximum gamut

I become rapture-gawker of fresh infinity consciousness
— and to think, I could have missed the whole show
the secret party while sapiens rest
missed the humblification, awestruck
beneath a glimmering, galactic starscape

after sound coating pine cones
I throttle the tent shut
zip out the flurry
and cocoon in for the night
but the wind keeps signaling me through the fabric
wanting to make me its smash kite
rainfly for my tail

MOTHER

mother artist sculpts the next generation
embedding seeds in the walls of her own body
reborn melon of life
broken apart and somehow made whole again

her verse is written across humanity's pages
she has published in every single one of us
the originator of text
and our first sounds of life

MÃE

mãe artista esculpe a próxima geração
semeando sementes em seu próprio corpo
melão de vida na barriga, quebra
e faz inteira novamente

seu verso está escrito nas páginas da humanidade
ela publicou em cada um de nós
a criadora de textos
e as primeiras batucadas de nossa vida

SINGLE MOTHERHOOD IS A PARTY

after decades, the cast of characters
strapped on shoes, bridled up
their wind horses to fly

what I'm saying is:
my children moved away
looking forward, as one must

unaccompanied, I inherited a red bicycle
spent evenings with the sunset
courted the public library,
the beach, the park

single motherhood is a party of activity
then extreme quiet

I put out bird seed to attract new songs
fill the hummingbird feeder with sugar water
tap on my own shoulder
saying thank you
and how are you on this fine day?

beloved artisan of creation and resilience,
what new canvas can we paint tonight?

3.

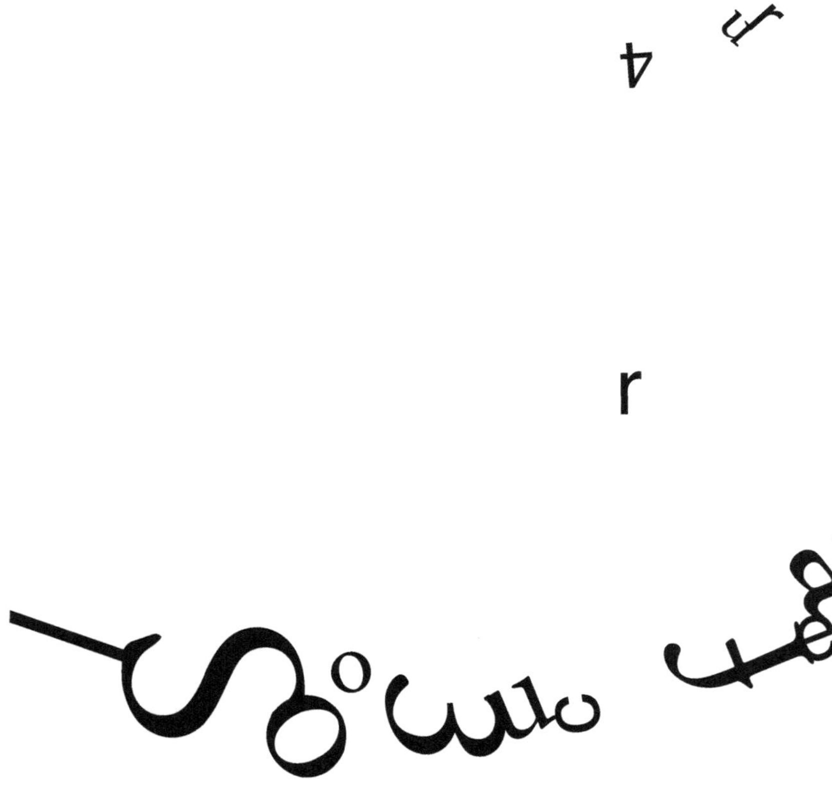

3/4 of Our Surface

FEATHER PSALM 56

I find a hollow feather

long as an open book

wind animates the artifact of flight

lifting it from the sand into the sky

we move together along the shore

sharing one shadow

long curved quill, emerging

from the tip of a human hand

PLUMA SALMO 56

encuentro una pluma hueca

largo como un libro abierto

el viento anima el artefacto del volar

levantándolo de la arena hacia al cielo

andamos juntos por la orilla del mar

compartiendo una sola sombra

una pluma larga y curvada, emergiendo

de la punta de una mano humana

PESALEME YA LESIBA 56

ke fumana siba le sekoti

le le lelele jwale ka buka e ahlameng

moya o pheula sefofi sena

o se nyolla lehlabatheng,
o se kopanya le lehodimo

re tsamaya mmoho lebopong, nna le siba lena

re arolelana moriti

motsu o kobeileng wa hlaha

o tswa ntlheng ya monwana wa motho

Sesotho translation by Katleho Kano Shoro & Pulane Mary Shoro

SUNSET IN OYA'S SAND STORM

for Reva

a flock of gulls levitate
sky surfing the same pitch of wind

invisible architect of everywhere air
lifts cloth & hair in all directions

particulates attack, sand waves bury shells
burrow into beaks, ears & eyes

terns plant their feet in wet earth
twist their heads away from the crackling surf

human children launch scoops of sand
in a raucous dialogue with the sea

my daughter sits in meditation
beside the lifeguard station, eyes shut

conducting the opus of orange juice concentrate
as it melts into the horizon

INSTABILITY

above the lagoon
a bow legged heron wobbles
on an electric wire
tightrope triangular
off balance
forgetting it has wings

THE BIGGEST MAMMAL ON EARTH WAS HERE

pass the olive lichen
trembling from pine branches

walk west
breathe in
the saline scent

green waves fill + empty + fill + empty
kelp beds slick with algae & surf grass

curl the body down
to greet the tidepool

skittering crabs & starburst
constellations of anemones

there —
beside the paprika sea star

a chunk of charcoal whale baleen
from inside the giant's mouth

CEMETERY | CEMENTERIO | CEMITÉRIO

light flickers off tiny shells,
sun illuminates what's broken
brittle shards of mollusks
that navigated oceana, now abandoned
the sea spits them out
to shine along the shore
reborn as glitter
treasures of refracted light

la luz del sol parpadea las conchas pequeñas,
ilumina lo que está roto
fragmentos frágiles, cáscaras secas de moluscos
que una vez navegaron el mar, ahora abandonados
oceana las escupe
que brillan a lo largo de la costa
renacidos como tesoros
brillantina de luz refractada

a luz do sol piscam nas conchas pequenas,
ilumina o que está quebrado
fragmentos frágeis, cascaras secas de moluscos
que uma vez navegaram oceana, agora abandonados
o mar cospe as conchas
que brilha ao longo da costa,
renascidos como tesouros
purpurina de luz refratada

VILLANELLE FOR YEMỌJA

ocean holds all languages in her expansive reach
dark silver nights, or crab shell mornings
she connects every continent

I arrive on foot, the gulls with wings
communing at the source of every syllable
ocean holds all the languages in her expansive reach

swirling emerald motion
seabirds hover, skitter on quick-canudo legs
she connects every continent

pelicans glide along her flat surface
sea lions lift their heads, gulp air
ocean holds all the languages in her expansive reach

curling waves become frothing foam
my body, a human form aging in slow motion
while the aquatic shapeshifter, connects every continent

water knows water, H20 & salt-to-salt
tidal-roll-crash-rumble
ocean holds all the languages in her expansive reach
she connects every continent

Translated from salt water

VILLANELLE PARA YEMỌJA

el mar abraza todos los idiomas en su alcance
noches plateadas y oscuras, o mañanas de concha-cangrejo
ella conecta todos los continentes

yo llego a pie, las gaviotas con alas
nosotros comuna en la fuente de cada sílaba
el mar abraza todos los idiomas en su alcance

movimiento esmeralda, arremolinado
las aves marinas flotan, o se deslizan sobre patas-de-popote
ella conecta todos los continentes

más allá, los pelícanos se deslizan por su superficie plana
los leones marinos levantan la cabeza, tragan aire
el mar tiene todos los idiomas en su alcance expansivo

las ondas rizadas se convierten en espuma
mi cuerpo, forma humana de envejecimiento lento
mientras la cambia formas acuática, conecta todos los continentes

agua conoce agua, H20 y sal-con-sal
maremotos-rolan, tumba-reketumba-elonga
el mar abraza todos los idiomas en su alcance
ella conecta todos los continentes

Traducido del agua salada

VILLANELLE RI TSJÁLA YEMỌJA

Jè ndáchikon tsabàkjá ngaijie énná jòkji chó nga ' ñóla̱
Ninga jñò ninga fate kji ni̱tje̱n, jòkji chrja̱ba̱la̱ nátsjá nga tajñò
Jè ndáchikon ' yajtín ngaijie a̱sànde̱

An ndsa̱koà fícho̱nia k ' o̱a̱ cho̱nndá jngála chóni
Jñá tii̱jòjtián ñà nchra̱báni jngò én
Jè ndáchikon tsabàkjá ngaijie énná jòkji chó nga ' ñòla̱

' ñó bítji tjo̱ sa̱se̱ ri tjín jìn nndá
Jñà nise ri ya̱ tjíma sa k ' o̱a̱ ta bímasòng ' a k ' o̱a̱ k ' enga majìn
ta ndsa̱ko fisonni nndá
Jè ndáchikon ' yajtín ngaijie a̱sánde̱
' ñó kjìn bímasòng ' a jñà cho̱ ng ' aísin ñani chrj ' ae chòn
Jñà cho̱ i ri tjín jin nndá kjo̱mìtje̱n jko̱ nga ' bì tjo̱
Jè ndáchikon tjínla̱ ngaijie én jokji kjìn chó nga ' ñòla̱

Jè tjo̱xila̱ nndá xóla̱ nndáchikon ma
Je̱ ijona̱ tafi tafi tímajchá, joni tsa jngò xi̱ta̱
Ñani o ' sín tíbatjìya jè nndáchikon ri ' ya ngaijie a̱sánde̱

Jè nndá fikj ' aá xakjín, H2O k ' o̱a̱ jè na̱xa̱ k ' o̱a̱ti̱ fikj ' aá xakjín
bítji tjo̱xkónla̱ nndáchikon k ' enga fane xkón fane ' ña
Jè ndáchikon tsabàkjá ngaijie énná jòkji chó nga ' ñòla̱
Jè ndáchikon ' yajtín ngaijie a̱sánde̱

Enná/Mazateco translation by Gloria Martinez Carrera

BEACH WITH MARKINGS

calm morning   beneath a white lace sky

the seashore becomes school for unlearning

this devoted student   arrives each day
notebook lined & pencil sharpened

the wind's enduring presence
jostles everything I possess

I leave
behind
the pinwheel
of a life
& am greeted   by the arc
of everything —

< best poem

4.

Undergrowth

APPROVED PORTABLE OXYGEN

we float above the forest's thick scalp

nose to the oval window
I study the topographical crazy quilt of our earth

while turbines & metal wings
catapult bodies & belongings across time zones
I pencil-in poems for exit seats

from a cloud's point of view
lakes are left-handed drawings of seahorses
alluvial rock typography

an avid reader, I will never tire of sky watching

HEMIPTERA

— Blue ridge forests are home to 158 tree species,
the largest variety in NorthAmerica.

I was born into a concrete city
with engineered rows of curated botanicals
we raise our young underground, sap-sucking commodities
oblivious to the box

the sound of the forest is new to me
novel is the night without an ambulance
siren, helicopter, or highway patrol
novel is the night without electrification

when I first heard the moon glow above the blue ridge mountains
the sky was plump with darkness
deafening chorus of 1.4 billion cicadas
calling for their mates

I zombie-walk to edge of the grove
to record the insect orchestra on my cell phone.
what's wrong with her, a child says to her mom
she's never heard the night before.

PERSPECTIVE

I

am

infinitesimal

breath

beating

inside

a

massive

biome

ARACHNID CHOREOGRAPHY

into the shelves

up the wall then back down again

I crawl onto the floor.

HAIKUS FOR A MILLIPEDE

the diplopoda
undulates 400 legs
skating the gray floor

sausage finger form
narceus americanus
venomous mouth claw

I search for something
to scoop it up, please go, no
cohabitation

carry it outside
in a white piece of paper
anything will do

open wide the door
set the creature down outside
close the door again

job done, that's enough
hydrogen cy-nide can burn
if you are threatened

millipede returns
beneath the door it enters
no-no-no-no-no

this time, toss it far
block the door gap with a mat
—but I'm the intruder

MARIMBA CHUVA

forest rain

drop

tap

tap-tip trat

trat

leaf pads

rain drop
splatters

sound

split

splot

timbal
play

droplets
tap

timbau
tap-tip trat
trat
leaf

pads

opal spot

drop
splatters
sound
split
splot

tap

tap-tip
trat-trat
iridescent

dots

tap-tip trat trat

leaf pads

drop

splatter

sound
split
splot

rain
plays
the
tree-timbales

ACCUMULATION

tiny raindrops
        can become
a downpour
        gotinhas de chuva
pode se tornar
        um aguaceiro
gotitas de lluvia
        puede llegar a ser
un aguacero
        tiny raindrops
can become
        a downpour
gotinhas de chuva
        pode se tornar
um aguaceiro
        gotitas de lluvia
puede llegar a ser
        un aguacero
tiny raindrops
        can become
a downpour
        gotinhas de chuva
pode se tornar
        um aguaceiro
gotitas de lluvia
        puede llegar a ser
un aguacero

ENCOUNTER WITH HORNETS

sunday —
hornet + cicada
one insect eats another
cicada = lunch

monday —
hornet + butterfly
four wings flutter on the dark pavement
butterfly = dinner

tuesday —
hornet + human
bug caught beneath a cup
that's for the butterfly!

PORTICO

a mother
wrapped in sleep
between a top
& bottom sheet

her dreams
open door after door
turning handles
passing thresholds

entering spaces
the city kept her
too occupied to reach

DOG KNOWS BEST

bullet the pitbull
refuses to return home
on a leash
after we've trounced
through the fecund forest

BETTY CREEK

for Ife

oh! her body
like a raft
in betty creek!

oh! her raft
beneath the sky
in a tree lined creek!

oh! her creek
sky surrounded
by trees!

oh! trees
her clothes
piled on a log!

oh! floating
on her back beneath
the tree canopy!

oh! creek!
oh! tree canopy!
oh! watering hole!

oh,
sky!
inside her body!

FLOCKING GESTURES

for Community of Writers

am /

filtered blue light rouses me
I land inside this body of sight

after six sleepless timeframes
I swallowed a whole chunk of night

prostrate before a glass rectangle
I study the green & black mountain range

trees are flocking along the ridge

pm /

after sabbath, before havdalah
ink slingers gather at sundown

our sonic field of communion begins
with croaking amphibians

we still our bodies so gallons of gilled stars
can swim into our ears

words flock inside us

BLACK WOMAN OF SOUND

for v

black woman of sound she named herself
gathering tones inside her chest

black   as in a grandparent's love
that hydrates verdant forests

sound   as in the origin of all-souls
vesseling ancestral with her wrists

cling, cling, clang
ping, clang, cling

watch me, she sang
her music orange-bright

cling, clang, cling
ping, pong, clang

nothing I don't believe in
is capable of obstacling

faith bursts boundaries
opens paths

before her   electric blue butterflies
around her   freedom floating fresh & sweet

MUJER NEGRA, SONORA

mujer negra sonora ella se nombró a sí misma
reuniendo tonos dentro de su pecho

negra   como el amor de abuelos
que hidrata bosques verdecentes

sonora   como el origen de todas las almas
corre la fuerza ancestral en su pulso

cling, cling, clang
ping, clang, cling

mírame, ella cantó
su música naranjada-brillante

cling, clang, cling
ping, pong, clang

nada en lo que no creo
es capaz de obstaculizar

la fe rompe fronteras
abre caminos

ante ella   mariposas azul-eléctricas
a su alrededor   la libertad flotando fresca y dulce

MULHER NEGRA, SONORA

mulher negra sonora ela se auto denominou
reunindo tons dentro do peito

negra   como o amor de avós
que hidrata florestas verdejantes

sonora   como a origem das almas
a força ancestral corre em seu pulso

cling, cling, clang
ping, clang, cling

olha para mim, ela cantou
sua música cor de laranja-brilhante

cling, clang, cling
ping, pong, clang

nada em que eu não acredite
é capaz de obstaculizar

fé ultrapassa limites,
abre caminhos

antes dela   borboletas azuis elétricas
arredor dela   a liberdade flutua fresca e doce

5.

Gravitational Fields

'NAME' IS AS GOOD A TERM AS ANY FOR AN UNTHINKABLE CONCEPT

96% of all that is the universe
is not anything we can remotely understand.
—Neil Degrasse Tyson

12.12 accelerated parabola & hyperbola of too hot time

11.11 swim though the equilibrium particle soup

10.10 located between 90 degrees & 270 degrees

9.9 this thing started as broken symmetry

8.8 particles are created in pairs, light is what happens

7.7 when matter & antimatter don't annihilate

6.6 lunch theory of string spaghettification

5.5 large becomes small in a zero energy universe

4.4 quantum foam & the fabric of space time

3.3 unthinkable accommodation to our ignorance

2.2 generate a term for life

1.1 by propelling yourself skyward at 7.6 mph

0.0 one mistake can trigger an entire universe from nothing

א

the first letter
of my name
has no sound

h (head) ouse

the second letter
of the aleph bet is
the first of beresheet
in the beginning

(let) ters

call out
to all mother
tongues

w (or) ds

ת

TA'AMIM AUTOCORRECTS AS GERANIUM

For Yonasan

Ta'amim are marks that indicate how the Hebrew language should be chanted. Abjad languages, like Hebrew and Arabic, are made of all consonants. Vowels are diacritics that often don't appear in text because fluent speakers have memorized them. This can be disorienting for readers accustomed to Latin script. How do you read without vowels? That question inspired this poem. The first part appears with only consonants, and the second with consonants and vowels.

1.

whn smn lss
thr trn f thght,
thy bbl

w'v bn bbblng
fr thsnds f yrs
xld frm r lngg & frms.

ttmpt t rd
b rd   I mn sng
th shm

'v bn syng
th shm vr m chldrn fr 30 + yrs

th shm s
ws nd wll b

th tchr sys hshm
nstd f dn, wh?
thr r mn nms fr [. . . .]
n fr wrk
n fr tchng
n fr fml

wrt n m ntbk
lhm s th wrd
w s n tm nd spc
drng r knwn xstnc

lttrs, dgsh
vwls & trps
r srvnts th snd
'm tng td
bfr thm,
lltrt t my mthr's
frst lngg

bt whn w sng
r vcs bnd
lk wtr   fmlr
bk   bbblng

2.

when someone loses
their train of thought
they babel

we've been babbling
for thousands of years
exiled from our languages & forms

I attempt to read
the shema
by read I mean sing
I've been speaking
the shema over my children for 30 + years,

the shema is
was and will be

the teacher says hashem
instead of adonai, why?
there are many names for [. . . .]
one for work,
one for teaching
one for family

I write in my notebook
elohim is the word
we use in time and space
during our known existence

letters, dagesh
vowels & tropes
are servants to the sound
I'm tongue tied before them,
illiterate to my mother's
first language

but when we sing
our voices bend
like water   familiar
a brook   babbling

THE LOCATION OF WORMS

—after the Akdamut

את	praise unceasingly	א
את	almost unintelligeble oneness	ב
את	all ages walking, crawling	ג
את	sometimes running, sleeping	ד
את	on the wings of all kinds	ה
את	starting with the angels	ו
את	of eggplant, hummus	ז
את	and shakshuka	ח
את	the angels of rest	ט
את		י
את	calendar year of praise	כ
את	rising up & down	ך
את	in all directions	ל
את	praise for good deeds	מ
את	be strong & courageous	ם
את	prayers for praise itself	נ
את	bird sung praises	ן
את	piyyut of praise	ס
את	even in the location	ע
את	of worms	פ
את	a woman could raise herself	ף
את	in sound & form	צ
את	singing with	ץ
את	the al-pha-bet	ק
את	until	ר
את	there was only	ש
את	quiet	ת

WHAT IF I WERE?

(as I actually am)

belonging to
the iron earth
(I pulse)

fluid torso
of rain
(I pour)

electric spine
of thunder
(I tremble)

weightless
limbs of air
(I levitate)

what if I were?
(exactly, as I am)

מה אם הייתי?

(כמו שאני בעצם)

אני שייכת

ל אדמח ברזל
(אני זורמת)

גוף נהר
של גשם נוזלים
(אני שופכת)

עמוד שדרה
חשמלי של רעם
(אני רועדת)

חוסר משקל
גפיים של אוויר
(אני מרחפת)

מה אם הייתי?
(בדיוק כמו שאני)

Hebrew translation by Bruria Finkel

الأرض الواقعية

(جذورنا النحاسية متسللة)

إلى نطفة أعماقنا
إلى نواة أجداعنا

(تنهمر علينا مبانينا الخيالية)

تصعقنا كهرباء أفقية المدى
(تسللت إلى منتصف العمر)

ذبذبات عديمة اللون والطعم
صارخة لعناية ألوهية
تمطر وتضحك في أفق واحد
(ماذا لو لم تكن)

دخان ها قد مضى كأن لو كان ولو برك
(تحت سحابة نارية الشظى)

أرجو ألا تعود تلك الومضة المالحة
(عسى؟)

Arabic translation/adaption by Hashel Lamki

NDE GRA BUI NGU DI NE?

(ga bui ngu
mahyegi di beni)

dri mengu ra bojahai
(di ngani)

ra xuthadehe ri ua'i
(ma ngok'ei dri pigi)

ra ntso ñ'uxutha ra gangay'e
(di huätsi
ma ndoy'o)

ya ma'ye ra ndähi
(ga rats'i)

¿nub'u ga bui ngu di ne?
(ngu majuäni to'ogi)

Hñähñu / Otomi translation by Margarita León

¿Y SI YO FUERA?

(exactamente,
como soy)

pertenezco a la tierra
de hierro
(yo vibro)

torso liquido
de lluvia
(me derramo)

eléctrica columna vertebral
de trueno
(yo tiemblo)

extremidades ligeras
de aire
(me elevo)

¿si yo fuera ?
(precisamente,
quien soy)

ANO KAYO KUNG AKO'Y?

(tunay na
talagang ako)

kabahagi ng
lupang bakalin
(pumipintig)

tuluy-tuloy na katawan
ng ulan
(bumubuhos ako)

ako'y kuryenteng
galugod ng kulog
(nanginginig)

walang timbang na
mga galamay ng hangin
(lumulutang)

paano kung ako'y?
(walang kulang, talagang ako)

Tagalog translation by Jilly Canizares

NA Sɛ ANKA MEYE?

(sɛnea mete ankasa)

na asase yi ayɛ sɛ dade ne me tenabea;
me de me ho ahyɛ asase yi mu
(me bɔ, te sɛ akoma)

nsu a efi nsu mu
(metow gu)

aprannaa bobom,
na anyinam tete gya yerɛwyerɛw
(m'ani wosow)

mframa a ano yɛ den ɛbɔ wɔ nan ho
(me sensɛn wim)

na sɛ anka mene?
(sɛnea mete ara)

Twi translation by A'bena Awuku Larbi

もしもわたしがそうだったなら？

(じっさいそうであるように)

てつの大地に
ぞくする
（わたしは脈うつ）
雨の流動体
（わたしはそそぐ）
かみなりの
エレクトリック・スパイン
（わたしはふるえる）
おもみなき
気体の手足
（わたしはうきたつ）
もしわたしが
（ありのままのわたしであるように）

Japanese translation by Kio Griffith

શું? કદાચ હું હોત !

(જેવી, હું ખરેખર છું)

કઠણ/કઠોર,લોખંડી પૃથ્વી સાથે
બંધાયેલી
(હું ધડકુ)/(હું ધબકુ છું)

ભિંજાયેલુ આ માથા વગરનુ શરિર
(હું મુસળધાર વરસુ છું

કરોડરજ્જુની ઇલેક્ટ્રિક ગર્જના
(હું ધ્રૂજું છું)

હવાના વજનહીન અંગો
(હું હવામાં ઉડીજઉ)

જો હું હોત તો?
(બરાબર, જેવી છુ તેમ)

Gujarati translation by Robin & Rajen Sukhadia with Girish Patel

或許過去的我正如現在的我一樣?

「正如我一樣」

屬於

堅毅的地球

「我的脈搏在跳動」

我的軀幹像雨水, 默默流動

「我傾瀉了」

電是雷的脊梁

「我顫抖著」

四肢失重

在空氣中飄蕩

「我懸浮」

或許過去的我正如現在的我一樣？

「確切, 正如我一樣」

Traditional Chinese translation by Janice Ngan

ET SI J'ÉTAIS?

(comme je suis réellement)

appartenant à
la terre de fer
(mon cœur bat)

le torse ruisselant
de pluie
(je suis une averse)

une colonne vertébrale à la puissance
du tonnerre
(je tremble)

les membres légers
comme de l'air
(je plane)

et si j'étais ?
(exactement,
comme je suis)

French translation by Patron Henekou

NE ÐE ME LE

(abe ale si me dzɔ
tututu la)

me dzɔ tso
ganyikɔ me
(dzinye le ƒoƒom)

tsi ƒo nye ametsia
le srasram yoyooyo
(tsi dzadzae me nye)

nye dzimeƒu hɔ ŋusẽ
akonka tso Só ŋtɔ gbɔ
(me le ƒoƒom titiiti)

abɔ kple afɔ fo
abe aya ene
(me le dzodzom
yina ɖe yame)

ke ne ɖe mele
(abe ale si tututu
mele ene)

Ewe translation by Patron Henekou

MIXOLYDIAN

Where does a mother tongue go when it isn't spoken?
Does it hide at the back of your throat?

Start a new conversation.
Choose a letter, said the א ב

Hay que comenzar
en algún lugar.

Da direita ou
da esquerda?

Los dos.

Cuantas lenguas? Inglês,
Espanhol, o Hebreo?

No importa.
Historia fluye
en todas las
direcciones.

Forward & also
back to open hands

סבבה!

Bueno, pues.

Ótimo.
Vou. Vamos.

Choose a letter, said the א ב

ב for beresheet?

לא
צ?

צ for wisdom?

Tampoco.

Começamos com
o mais pequeno.

כן

kotzo shel yod.

י

י

is a fingerprint
tiny mark
burning through the dusk
to enunciate

first rain of winter
a primeira chuva
do inverno
יחס

yachas
relación
relaçao

יעד
yaad
goal & destination
mi meta
nossa destinaçao
porta aberta
paisagem da conexão

ישר
yashar
honest, go forward

claro

יותר
י
יייייייייי
יייייייייייייי
small
salival
som
לה
פונטה
דל יד
she reads Spanish
inside the Hebrew letters
vessels of multiple migrations

י

ı

gathers
glottal notes
at the back of
throat

ı

יברית

ı

ידיש

ı

Ge'ez.

Ladino.

la punta del yud
finds sanctuary
at the roof of your keter

ı

el sonido más chico que
la posibilidad
saudação
de som
o ser entendida
dona da respiração
propia
sou e somos

קיצת

mini

mais mayor que
o tamanho de
um bujão

אתה

chiquitica

sonic swallow
a continuação
de som
que somos   sim
som sambando
silencios sonicôs
sambão sempre

no hay que
discutir

potentialities

sua boca
e a minha
eu
nos
ela   el
ella o allah
ainda sim, em circunstâncias que
circumvent espaços geográficos
diásporas atômicas
multilingues polifônicas
palabras
- anônimas
יברית
espaços especias
inhabit the back
of throat

yo   yes   ypsom   ee gree eh gah   gar

גם אני
גם

את   אתה   א

such sounds

começam com

heat of liquid air
the spit catheter
of
ancient prayer

יפה

yafa, yafe, yafim, yafot

yafa, yafe, yafim, yafot

letras

sea of sound

ירוק

yaroch

verde, *te quiero verde*

como el

ים

amelach

THANK YOU SO MUCH FOR LISTENING

This found poem is made of fragments in a Zoom chat during a poetry workshop with Brenda Hillman. The chat included Brenda, Stephanie Anagnoson, Jill Bergantz, Tawanda Mulalu, Tova Green, Paul Nelson, Jeannie Koops-Elson, Yeva Johnson, Ellene Glenn Moore, Lester Lennon, Shahrzad Moshiri, and Maria Guzman.

the aerodynamics of the poem
upgrades to a higher level of seeing
sets me up for creepiness

this beautiful human quilt
can go in several directions
lead along on a path labyrinth-ing

I began with a mind
a quote, and a definition
skin and kin and kind

tracing back the word
we know as human love
roots connected to each other

in a microsomal way
crepuscular stampede
of em dashes and semicolons

learnedness and conversation
knowledge — like talking to someone
who is excited to be there

a title becomes exactly how we think
epigraphs
and starting points

paratactic consciousness
one thing put next to each other
as opposed to disjointed hypotactic

we connect and don't connect
little praiselettes
phraselettes

travel from one real thing to another
an interlocutor willing to go
anywhere — the IP address

the social security card
tongues hanging out
with different kinds of knowing

fast and loose, unflinching
the linen, the knot, the big space poem
now 100 years old

exactly the same manager
of a record store, compassion
and awe elevate a simple observation

who and where we are
giving to the doormat
afflicted, I can imagine

worlds, traditions, families
different views, making order
incomprehensible

a gauze, trance-brewed suspension
of belief, asks you to accept
what you can't understand

I had committed to writing scatter
when it comes to violence
you can't out violence the monster

this insane mom-thing takes over
yet I'm too old
I couldn't stop their arms

stop
the naming
of everything

you are looking at a trunk
that's a dream, branches
coming out of my mouth

WHAT IS BEING BORN INSIDE YOU?

naked feet on wet porcelain
water pours onto my back

body bent, I am trying
to save two precious things

from slipping
down the drain

a sparrow, small as a wish
its saturated feathers floundering

& an egg the size of an olive
too small to sit up on its own

awake all night
the dream marauder says:

never underestimate the power of the weak

I FLY

I had a really wild dream .... a really good dream ....
.... there are all these ...... different parts to it I
am so glad to remember my dreams .... I was on the beach ....
.... a guy was wearing a coat with
wings .... and ....
he was just flapping his jacket sleeves ....
.... he could rise up .... and fly along the shore ....
.... I looked at him .... and I was thinking ....
.... I could totaly do that .... when I saw .....
the .... um .... man .... flying ....
.... I knew I could do it .... because ....
.... I - do - it - all - the - time ....
.... I know to flap my arms .... and just ...... fly ....
and now that I'm awake and thinking of the dream ....
.... it's bc I fly all the time in my
dreams .... I levitate ....
.... I don't actually
know how to do that. Ha! ..... in my waking life .... but
I knew in the dream .... that I do it all the time ....
.... and I do it without even a coat that has big wings ....
so now I know that I fly .... I kind of .... just ....
. levitate .... and I like to .... rise up
.... and look out over the situation ....
AND I ALWAYS KNOW HOW TO RISE UP ....
.................I fly all the time! .... so this guys comes down .... he ....
comes right .... above me .... he starts to fall ....
.... he does this as a mean joke ....
.... to see if I'd become scared ... he would squish me ....
and I'm like .... whatever dude ....
.... you have your fancy coat ....
.... but - I - fly - all - the - time! ....
.... I was like .... OK
..... I'll give it a try .... I know I could do this .... bc I do
this .... all ... the ... time ....

sure enough .... I took off ....
....
.... and I started flying all around the beach ....
....
I went to the top of the sky ....
....
.... I put my hand around the side of the curtain ....
....
and I touched the space beyond the sky ....
....
.... cause it was almost like a theater stage for a show ....
.... and there was an end to it ....
....
.... and that was pretty good for the first time I came back ...
and put something inside a cabinet on the sand ....
.... I remember feeling really hurt in my heart ....
.... but on the other hand .. I remembered that I knew how to fly! ......
....
.... I could see ... touch behind the ceiling ....
.... the highest heavenly place ....
.... and see the game of it all ....
....
there were events happening .... films .... and .... rooms ....
.... but we didn't have a guide ....
.... I didn't know how to get there, where I needed to go ....
.... or even find out what was possible ....
I was in a room .... with .... people ....
..... there was something going on ....
.... there were people writing on the walls ....
..... like on a big poster .... and just ...... complaining ....
.... about EVERYTHING ....
complaining complaining complaining ....
....
.... but I looked more closely at the room ... and I said ....
....
.... look everyone .... lets just come together ....
.... let's sit down ....

....
on the table was a big poster for examination ....
.... when I read it .... carefully ....
and [long ass silence] .... [swallow] .... [more silence] ......
....
when I read it .... carefully ....
it was not a poster about complaints ....
.... when I looked at it very very closely ....
....
.... It was a topographical map of the planet ....
....
.... It was about the water and the land ....
....
and the meaning was ....
.... peace ....
....
.... and this was the peace ....
.... this was the peace ...... room ....
....
....
... and I had read the whole wall wrong ....
.... I thought it was a place
where everyone was ....
....
complaining about how nothing was done right ....
.... everything is corrupt ....
everything falls short .... but ....
.... actually ....
.... it was an enormous poster the size of a table ....
with a bunch of people around it ....
.... we put our hands on the table ....
.... it was a 3D topographical map of the planet ....
.... the land and the water ....
....
and the whole point ...... of this session ....
....
.... was .... peace ....

SHE OPENED HER MIND

& the dream was already
inside there
behind the left rib-rack
above the kidneys
round-abouting her lymph
attic, system purring
the word yessssssssssss

what lives
inside the sound
of a woman?

stories, that burn obstacle lists
fire, that can obliterate the age-old willingness
to hold anyone's hand
but your own

CALCULATIONS^3

$$\frac{\text{surviving}}{\text{electric}} \quad + \quad \frac{\sqrt{\ }\text{storms}}{\text{shadows}} \quad / \quad \text{(earth's surface)}$$

(×) = orbiting pear

RANDOM EXPERIMENTS IN BIOLUMINESCENCE

Imagine a mass of stars with the magnitude of space & the value of one.

Ponderable space & finite matter interact at a value of zero.

Locate a pregnant question in the context of the infinite universe
inside a woman's body.

Factor in the rigid bodies of her antecedents, progeny and futures.

If she is positioned in contexts of inertia,
institutions in bounded space will have a dampening effect.

Her actions become reduced to carbon.

This is common among homo sapiens
but extremely irregular in star matter
due to the scope of gravitating mass & incalculable velocities.

Luminescence is equal in practice everywhere
as expressed in the phenomena of light,
empty space in local time
including clock time — whether X or X prime.

A rigid body almost always corresponds with its shadow.

Shadow figures touch and their shadows also touch.
A shadow can become infinitely great
propagating in persistent schematic arrangements.

How can the universe inside a woman's body become infinite
when she is located in contexts where there is no room?

- Abstract figures in the continuum from two to six dimensions.

- Assume spherical space that departs
  from standard measurements.

- Shift conditions to envision all points, planes, shadows
  all spheres coinciding with each other.

- Envision the woman's body unbounded.

By changing gravitational fields in tangible space

the woman's body becomes

a luminous

point .

Download the SoundCloud App, and Scan the QR codes below to listen to playlists of select performances in the Orality Archive.

Plurilingual Hybrid Poems

1 Poem in 11 Languages

Poems in Local & International Languages

ORALITY ARCHIVE

Poems: Location of Worms
Mixolydian [English, Español, יברית]

Poet: Amy Shimshon-Santo (as^{2})

Poem: What If I Were?

Poets: as^{2} [English, Español]
A'bena Awuku Larbi [Twi]
Margarita de León [Otomi / Hñähñu]
Bruria Finkel [Hebrew]
Hashel Lamki [Arabic]
Jilly Canizares [Tagalog]
Kio Griffith [Japanese]

Poems: 1000 Bird Tree
Residence | Terrestre | Guaa' 'vö
Feather Psalm 56 | Pluma Salmo 56 | Pesaleme Ya Lesiba 56
Villanelle For/Para Yemanja | Villanelle Ri Tsjála Yemanja

Poets: as^{2} [English, Español]
Eleuterio Xagaat García [Chinanteco]
Katleho Kano Shoro & Pulane Mary Shoro [Sesotho}
Gloria Martinez Carrera [Enná/Mazateco]
Àkpà Árinzèchukwu [Nigerian Pidgin]

OPTIONAL CORNELL NOTES FOR H SAPIENS

Dr. Eliud "Eddie" Partida

Pollination: "Pollination relies on the reproduction of plants, and flowering plants rely on the relationship that we call symbiosis — where both organisms benefit and are actually in relationship and rely on each other for that specific species to survive and thrive. We think of pollination to reproduce. Bees are doing this —not for the plant— but they are benefitting from the nectar of the flower and use this to make honey for their colony. The flower is manifested to make more beautiful flowers and colors to continue that coevolution. Bees become more specialized in extracting honey, and the flowers become more specialized in attracting pollinators. It's a result of millions of years of this co-relationship to become what it is to develop into the beautiful relationship called pollination."

Proximity: "Biologically, proximity affects the terms of exchange. Cells that are close to each other exchange information by exchanging chemical signals and electrical signals. Proximity allows them to communicate with each other at the small cellular level, but that transmits into more macro behavior that we use to interact with the world. Our proximity to each other also dictates our relationships between each other and nature, and the physical spaces between us. Proximity allows me to see the relationship I have biologically with others, and other living things. 'Out of sight is out of mind' is really true. Unless I am close to, and in close relationship with, I don't see how I am connected to everything — even though I am."

Gravitational Fields: "Gravitational fields have to do with how things are attracted to each other, and, also, the size of these objects. Everything in the universe has an attractive force. We are on this planet because there is a force that pulls us to the center of the Earth. We call that gravity. We are also attracted to objects in the same way. Because of their size, we don't feel them as obvious, [but] there is attraction to all objects in that way."

ACKNOWLEDGMENTS & PROCESS NOTES

I am very grateful to the editors and curators who published and/or exhibited earlier versions of poems in this book.

"Art + Labor / Arte + Labor" appears in Tiltwest's Magazine Issue of the same name. Curated by Storm Ascher.

"Cemetery - Cementerio - Cemitério"; "Downpour," "Aguaceiro," "Black Woman of Sound, Mujer | Mulher Negra Sonora" *Everything Connection: Land, Body, Cosmos* curated by Miyo Stevens Gandara for Self Help Graphics & Art. Archived on Google Arts & Culture.

"Lemon" was commissioned by Invertigo Dance Theatre.

"Single Motherhood is a Party" appears in *Poetica: Writer's Anthology of Poetry*, Clarendon House Books, 2019.

"She Opened Her Mind," "Calculations," and "Random Experiments in Bioluminescence" appear in *Radical Wom!n: An Anthology of Non-Conformism* with DIO Press. Edited by Epifania Amoo-Adare and Rapti Siriwardane.

"Mixolydian" was commissioned by Shmutzik Shmates for "The Letters Project." Special thanks to Etai Rogers-Fett for the invitation and Avila Santo for his collaboration on the audio version.

A portion of "Thank You All For Listening" appears in *Reformatting the Painscale Anthology.*

"Villanelle for Yemanja" was commissioned for Universidad Autónoma Metropolitana (UAM) Unidad Cuajimalpa (95th Anniversary Honoring Miguel León Portillo). Curated by Delia Xóchitl Chavez and Cynthia Martinez Benavidez. It was first performed in English, Spanish, Mazateco, and Chinanteco for *Poesia Plurilingue* with Gloria Martínez Carrera and Eleuterio Xaggat Garcia.

Heartfelt thanks to everyone who helped bring this work to life. Bless the wonderful humans at Flowersong Press: Edward Vidaurre, Avery Castillo, Priscilla Celina Suárez, and my pressmates.

Pao Chutijirawong created the magical cover art for this book, and styled the figure on the front cover from a photograph taken of me playing in the park by Bobby Gordon. Gayle Brandeis was my first reader and laughed with me about translating the sea and bird song into human language. Gayle — along with Leonora Simonovis, Mamle Wolo, Adrian Ernesto Cepeda, Karen Llagas, and Angela Siew — read and commented on earlier versions of this manuscript offering helpful insights. Eddie Partida graciously spoke with me about pollination, proximity, and gravitational fields while we were co-teaching novice classroom teachers during the pandemic. Ife Williams invited me on an inspiring visit to the Hambidge Center in the Blue Ridge Mountains where we took long walks, threw ceramic pots, and I wrote insect and forest poems that now live in this book. Storm Ascher commissioned "art + labor/arte + labor" at a transitional time in my life when inclusion felt like a raft toward my next life. Epifania Amoo-Adare and Rapti Siriwardane didn't blink when I sent them experimental poems for an academic anthology. Miyo Stevens Gandara invited me to create audio performances for curatorial process with Self Help Graphics & Art. My son Avila mixed and mastered the audiobook, and this was no small feat since it included recordings made on every imaginable kind of microphone.

My wonderful children merit more than a few lines of thanks, so this is a placeholder for eternity. You are my life's greatest treasures. Big love to my family, friends, and all the continents where we live. You are my photosynthesis.

This collection is evidence of poetry as wayfinding. I am grateful for the life force within and around me. The process completely shifted my perspective on what kind of a writer I wish to be in the world at this time. The pandemic sent me outside, online into the virtual arms of global friends, and, eventually, out of the country. Close and far melted together. Playing across languages and contexts opened my mind. This journey guided me toward new visions for habitat, language, and community.

Delia Chavez welcomed me into her amazing mind, and numerous literary spaces throughout Mexico to participate in polylingual readings with Radio Educación Bilingüe, Universidad Autónoma Metropolitana, and UNESCO Rumbo Mondiacult. She also connected me to poets Eleuterio Xaggat García, Manuel Bolom, Juan Sant, and Gloria Carrera. I am deeply inspired by their perspectives, generosity, and language activism.

Simultaneously, I enjoyed numerous provocative conversations with Sabata Mokae and Mamle Wolo about mother tongue, education, and publishing. Some of the themes we discussed appear in our essay "Repatration of Language, Culture, and Community" in the first edition of the *Writers' Project Ghana Journal.*

Before long, Mamle read with us in Mexico, and opened spaces for polylingual poetry exchanges across the Atlantic at the Pa Gya! Literary Festival in Accra, Ghana. California, Accra, Lagos, Oaxaca, CDMX, and Bahia, Brasil came together. One year, Nana Asaase, Margarita de León, Gloria, and I translated each other's work for a panel Mamle titled "From Mazateco to Twi." The following year, Patron Henekou, Katleho Kano, and I translated our poems through English, French, Ewe, Sesotho, Spanish, and Portuguese. Some of these translations live inside this book as joyful memories. (I must also say that it's been an honor to work with Martin Egblewogbe on various Writers' Project Ghana projects, and I appreciate Efe Paul Azino's hospitality at LIPFEST.)

These experiences revealed the need for me to face my mother's mother tongue. She has sat with me to translate poems into her first language, Hebrew. Rabbi Yonason Perry had long weekly talks about Hebrew, the Sephirot, the Sefer Yetzirah, and ancient examples of Jewish poetics. Etai Rogers-Fett invited me to participate in The Jewish Letters Project where we all chose one letter to interpret through art. This gave rise to "the location of worms" and "mixolydian." I wrote "the location of worms" on my cousin Eyal's couch, and his partner Mirit kindly listed her favorite words that begin with the letter yud that appear in "Mixolydian."

The Community of Writers supported me to write and commune on the land. Monica Mills and Thomas Dunni early readers of the hybrid plurilingual poems. When I came up with the "Location of Worms," they asked, "How would you read that?" How indeed. I had no idea. It had to become a layered chant.

Marina Magalhães, Isis Avalos, and Tatiana Zamir pushed me to relax into play. They liked the sleepy, post-dream, voice note and the "genealogy of a moment" I brought into our dance rehearsals.

I've always longed to speak all of our family languages, including our ancestral ones. It's been difficult to try and read different symbols that move in different directions. Nothing is too difficult with exposure, but my schooling in the U.S. never included ancient languages. Abjad languages, like Hebrew and Arabic, are made of consonants. Vowels appear as markings (diacritical signs). Niqqud are unnecessary for fluent speakers, and are eventually removed from the text. Vowels are like training wheels on a bike. Additional markings, called ta'amim, tell the reader how to chant or sing a text. I've heard that this is also true in other ancient languages including Yoruba. This is evidence of the importance of orality and song in our literacy legacies.

My need for poetic forms relevant to multiple cultures erupted after realizing that my family's heritages were absent from standard study. I felt bereft. I called my mother and moaned, "Have we no poetic forms?" "What are you talking about?!" she said aghast. "Baruch ata adonai elohainu!" She began to pray over me. You see? We are made of poetry.

Because ancient languages are rarely taught in U.S. schools, restoring mother tongue requires taking a literary stance. This shifts authority from formal education to households and communities. We consult our elders as the experts. We reach out to family and friends.

Many people in the U.S. mourn "losing" our mother tongues, but we didn't just forget them behind the couch. Tremendous violence has taken place for one to "lose" a language. "Loss" is the outcome of systematic dispossession. Thankfully, people all over the world are organizing to honor languages as inheritance, and affirm plurilingualism.

As a writer and teacher, I've fretted over what to do about this. We can stop editing our languages out, and stop feeling ashamed of what we've "lost." I've learned that even one letter in an ancient language is a treasure. For example, in Hebrew, each letter has a specific gematria (numerology) and creation story. One letter is a world.

Plurilingual friends and family translated poems for this volume into their many familial languages. We includeded an Orality Archive (and made an audiobook) so that you can see and hear translations in their own voices. The translations include: A'bena Awuku Larbi (Twi), Kio Griffith (Japanese), Hashel Lamki (Arabic), Janice Ngan (Traditional Chinese), Jilly Canizares (Tagalog), Margarita de León (Hñähñu/Otomi), Robin and his father Rajen Sukhadia (Gujarati), and Patron Henekou (French, Ewe), Katleho Shoro Kano and her mum Pulane Mary Shoro (Sesotho), Gloria Martinez Carrera (Mazateco/Enná), Àkpà

Árinzèchukwu (Nigerian Pidgin), and Eleuterio Xagaat García (Chinanteco).

When copyediting this book, we choose not to list every language as a translation. Writing itself is an act of translating an experience or sentiment into language. For plurlingual people, languages often arrive together. We chose to list translations to honor the guest translators and the language they were inhabiting. We also referenced "translaiton" in the hybrid plurilingual poems for legibility.

When not indicated as a translation, the non-English poems were written by me. I am grateful for the conversations and gentle copyediting of Delia Chavez ("Pluma Salmo 56," and "Terrestre"), Pati Del Valle ("Arte + Labor, Cemíterio, Mujer Negra Sonora"), Gloria Martínez Carrera ("Villanelle Para Yemanja"), Margarita de León ("Y Si Yo Fuera"), Amen Santo ("Arte + Labor, Cementerio, Mulher Negra Sonora") and Ana Rita Santiago ("Mãe").

A tree will bend itself in search of light. So will a woman. She will lay down and crawl along the ground to find it. There is dirt beneath the fingernails of these poems. Writing has moved me to the oldest ground—the Earth. I feel deep respect for the natural world and awareness of our interconnectedness. Writing outside made me notice what was actuall happening around me. For example, "1000 Bird Tree" is a fictional response to a true story. My neighbors hacked down an enormous old tree and dug up its roots. It took a week of saws, trucks, and dumpster trips to remove it from the ground. I felt this violence viscerally, weeping at the massacre. The tree was older than any human in our neighborhood, and I'd been breathing its air for 20 years. It was also home to multiple species. Until that time, I'd imagined gentrification primarily as displacing people. Of course human settlements have destroyed animal habitats, changed waterways, and leveled terrain.

In my heritage, there are special holidays just for trees (Tu B'shevat) and times of year to eat outside (Sukkot). Kitchen tools are made kosher by placing them in the soil. We greet the new year with fruit and honey. On the African-Brazilian side of our family, divinity animates the oceans, rivers, plants, and sky. The natural world is central to one's personal identity and communal spiritual life.

Languages and habitat are intertwined. Earth-centered writing, living, and community organizing was espoused by Zitkala-Sa (Yankton Sioux, 1876-1938). Barry Lopez wrote that one can't understand place without local (indigenous) languages. The task of a writer during climate change, said Deena Metzger, is to restore the natural world to the human imagination. Writing with nature is not an escape. It is a return. We must come to know each other. Philosopher Olúfẹmi O. Táíwò advocates for translocalism as a response to the climate crisis.

Plurilingualism is natural to me, as it was for many of my ancestors. That's the migrants' predicament. You speak your family languages at home, and collect other languages where you work or study when you are displaced or need to move.

Systems are held in place by policies and laws. They are also kept in place by culture, languages, and by form. I began experimenting with poetic forms in Latin-based languages, but the shift to mother tongue exploded into songs, chants, or visual mandalas.

Mother tongue can change one's perspective on life itself. For example, in my friend Mamle's father's indigenous language Krobo, the word for woman and mountain are synonymous. There is a particular mountain that is known to be the mountain of her heritage. Now, wouldn't that change your sense of self, knowing that you were a mountain? In English, a "woman" is a subset of "man" while in Krobo she is a mountain, and a mountain is the keeper of her heritage. This is beautiful to me. It also demonstrates how words have different ontologies.

When I was a child, my mother used to speak in her first language with her family through a wall phone in the kitchen. She would move about tied to a receiver connected to a long, curly telephone wire. As a kid, I knew that our larger family existed somewhere else, and that they were living inside a different language that I never learned. Languages are operating systems that structure knowledge and codify experience. Not learning the language has been painful existentially. Growing up in California, and teaching students for decades, I know this is a pain shared by many children of immigrants.

The journey to restoring language is full of mysterious connections. Once, when I was studying the letter י (yud), I stumbled on an anti-patriarchal poem written by Yehuda Leib Gordon in 1878 called "Kotzo shel yod." The tip of the yud. The poem was translated into Ladino in 1901, and I first encountered the Ladino version as "לה פונטה די לה יוד" or "La punta del yod." (Even as I type this within an English sentence, you would be reading it backward.) When I slowly sounded out each Hebrew letter, Spanish sounds came out! La. לה Punta. פונטה

De La. לה די Yud. יד In the poem, Gordon (גורדון) decried Jewish women's social degradation by comparing us to the smallest letter of the alphabet — the י. We had no chance for autonomy, ownership, or self authorship. I doubt that he ever imagined a woman like me could exist, much less read his poem a century later. A woman who writes for herself. A woman who has been a head of household. This begs the question, what futures are we conjuring that might also seem unimaginable?

There are no perfect translations. Translation tries to bring one context into another. My family lives inside multiple contexts all the time. I am most ciomfortable without having to exclude any precious part. "Mixolydian" is how it feels to live inside my head. I am always weaving, and I imagine this is true for many, many, many people.

We are witnessing far too many examples of people dishonoring each other, normalizing abuse of power, and causing traumatic harm. The problem is not "the world" in general. The problem is specifically with our species. I desire a new anthem for the U.S. without rockets red glare or bombs bursting in air. Instead, let us learn to really listen and speak with each other. We will need all of our languages to begin to communicate authentically.

In both Hebrew and Arabic, conversations start by asking about peace. Shalom means peace. Salaam means peace. We greet each other: "how is your peace?" not "how are you?" We wish each other peace each time we meet, and when depart. Hello Peace. Goodbye Peace. You might never know this in light of current tragic circumstances. We must make peace. We can bring peace.

Toni Morrison wrote that the challenge of the 21st century would be whether or not we could create a shareable world. I want my life and words to help manifest shareability.

This collection is playful, but with serious intent. I play to disobey. I play to imagine other ways. There are over 7000 living languages on Earth right now and "the ocean holds all our languages in her expansive reach." These poems express their innate sense of belonging. If the Earth can hold all of our languages and cultures, why can't we?

Photo: Bobby Gordon

Amy Shimshon-Santo (Author) is a warm-blooded vertebrate with hair (H. sapien, genus Homo). Like other mammals, she has a cranial skeleton that connects the base of her skull to her backbone, pelvis, legs, feet, and toes. She belongs to the class Mammalia—of which there are 4500 different expressions on water, land, and in the air. Equipped with milk producing mammary glands, she birthed two punims and raised them into adulthood. Her small canine teeth chew food and the mouth whistles well. She has domesticated fire, refrigerators, and bathroom appliances including faucets and mirrors. Born in the Pacific Rim, her shallow time linguistic assets are plurilingual due to multiple migrations. Blood type 0. As of her last examination: her temperature was 98.1; respirations 19; diastolic 101, and diastolic 67. Audiologically, the hearing in her right ear was Type A / C-110 borderline negative and her left was Type A. Her word recognition scores were 100 %.

Pao Chutijirawong (Cover Artist) เกิดที่ประเทศไทย Asun nyt suomessa (born in Thailand and lives in Finland). Chutijirawong works in a multidisciplinary fashion using sculpture, video, performance, and new media. She was an artist in residence at the Hambidge Center (GA, USA) and Yale Norfolk (CT, USA). Previously based in Florida, USA, she earned a BFA in Fine Art with double minors in Graphic Design and Art History. Chutijirawong is currently pursuing a master's degree in Contemporary Design at Aalto University in Finland.

DEDICATION

This book is dedicated to all the languages of the Earth,
and to my family and friends who speak them.

I end / begin this volume by honoring the generations. This list of names starts with my children and reaches back in time. The family names appear in the languages they were first spelled in at birth. Most of my egun would have opened any book from this side, so I include this on what would be their first page.

Reva Aisha
Avila Eytan
Amy Ruth
ברוריה
David
פרידה רשקה
היים אליעזר
שלמה
ריבה
אברהם דוד
תמר אסטר
אברהם
בן
בסי
פיוטר
ברטה
ברינה
אלטר שלמה נכ
ישראל דב
דוד
מרדכי
סרה
מירה
שלמה

FLOWERSONG
PRESS

Flowersong Press nurtures essential verse from, about, and throughout the borderlands. Literary. Lyrical. Boundless.

Sign up for announcements about new and upcoming titles at

www.flowersongpress.com

www.ingramcontent.com/pod-product-compliance
Lightning Source LLC
Chambersburg PA
CBHW051627120626
46551CB00014B/1974
* 9 7 8 1 9 6 3 2 4 5 3 5 6 *